Presented to

_____

From

_____

Date

_____

Jesus Said

Bible Storybook

Jesus Said Bible Storybook

Copyright © 2003 Educational Publishing Concepts, Inc., Wheaton, IL

Published in Nashville, Tennessee, by Tommy Nelson, a Division of Thomas Nelson, Inc.

Scripture quotations are from the International Children's Bible® New Century Version®, © 1983, 1986, 1988, 1999 Tommy Nelson®, a Division of Thomas Nelson, Inc.

ISBN: 1-4003-0236-6

Printed in China

03 04 05 06 07 — 5 4 3 2 1

Jesus Said

Bible Storybook

Carolyn Larsen

Illustrated by
Rick Incrocci

NELSON®

www.tommynelson.com

A Division of Thomas Nelson, Inc.
www.ThomasNelson.com

TABLE OF CONTENTS

The Old Testament

New Testament

Dear Parents,

In the book of Colossians, Paul wrote: "Let the teachings of Christ live in you richly" (3:16).

There has been much talk in recent years about what Jesus would do in normal life situations and, further, what we should do to be more like Him. But this book is different. It's designed to help children know what Jesus said and how people throughout Scripture—in both the Old and New Testaments—modeled His teachings. By seeing Jesus' words played out in the lives of people like Noah, Moses, Esther, Zacchaeus, and Peter, children will see Jesus in all of God's Word.

They will learn what Jesus said about living for God and living in relationship with one another. They will see the Bible as one glorious book of God's divine plan, not as isolated historical events. Both Old and New Testament stories are told as practical lessons that illustrate the teachings of Jesus Christ.

At the end of each Bible story, you will have the opportunity to review with your children the lesson in light of "What Jesus Said" about the related concept.

My prayer for the children who read this book is that God will use these words and this format so that Christ's teachings will live in them richly throughout their lives.

Carolyn Larsen

The Story of Creation

The earth was empty in the beginning. There was no light—sun, moon, or stars. There were no trees or plants. No animals or bugs or birds. There were not even any people. There was nothing . . . except God.

All God had to do to make things was say the words. "Let there be light!" He said. Bright light filled the sky. God called the light time "Day." He called the dark time "Night." God did all of this on His first day of making things.

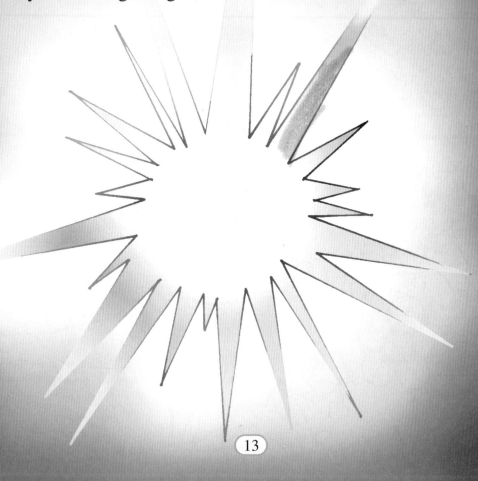

The second day God said, "Let there be space between the waters." A big space formed and He called it "sky." On the third day, God worked on the earth. He made mountains, deserts, rivers, and lakes. He filled the earth with trees, flowers, and plants of all kinds.

The fourth day God put the bright sun in the daytime sky. He made the twinkling stars and shiny moon for nighttime. The fifth day of creation must have been fun. God put fishes of all sizes and shapes in the waters. He made brightly colored birds to fly through the sky.

God started the sixth day of creation by making animals to run across the land. His last creation was the most amazing. God made man and woman. God looked around at everything He had made, and He was happy with all of it. So, on the seventh day, God rested.

WHAT JESUS SAID

God can do all things.
MATTHEW 19:26

God made something from nothing! No one else could do that. God made everything there is on earth, from the tiniest bug to the biggest mountain. He had incredible ideas, too. He made caterpillars that become butterflies, and He made animals that can change their skin color to protect themselves from their enemies.

Jesus said, "God can do all things." So, we know we can trust Him to help us with anything we need. There is nothing too hard for God!

Obeying Saves Noah

Many years passed and large numbers of people filled the earth. These people forgot God and began to do bad things. "I am sorry that I ever made people," God said. "They have stopped paying attention to Me. They do not obey Me anymore. They are not even nice to one another." Only one man still obeyed God. That man was Noah.

"A big flood is coming," God told Noah. "Everything on earth will be covered with water. But you will be safe if you do what I tell you to do." God knew that Noah still loved Him. He wanted Noah to be safe.

"Build a big boat. Make it exactly the way I tell you to build it," God said. Noah obeyed. He did what God said. When the big boat, called an ark, was finished, God sent lots of animals to go inside it. He sent two of every kind of animal on earth.

Noah and his family went inside the ark, too. Pretty soon Noah heard rain falling outside. It rained so much that water covered the ground and the ark began floating on the water. It rained for forty days and forty nights. The whole earth flooded, just as God said it would.

When the flood was over Noah and his family and all the animals came out of the ark. The first thing Noah did was thank God for keeping them safe. "Have babies and fill the earth with life again," God told Noah. He told the animals the same thing. "I promise I will never flood the whole earth again," God said. He put a rainbow in the sky as a sign of His promise.

WHat JESUS SaiD

Everyone who hears these
things I say and obeys
them is like a wise man.
MATTHEW 7:24

It wasn't raining when **God** told Noah to build the ark. But Noah was a wise man. He did what **God** said. He didn't ask **God** a lot of questions. He didn't argue with **God**. He just obeyed Him. Noah and his family would have drowned in the flood, just like everyone else, if Noah had not obeyed **God's** words.

We are wise when we obey **God's** words, too. The Bible tells us how **God** wants us to live. It tells us how Jesus lived His life. All we have to do is read His book and obey what **God** tells us. That will show that we are wise, too.

The Tower of Babel

At this time in history, everyone on earth spoke the same language. People could travel anywhere in the world and always be able to talk with the people they met. One group of people moved to a place in Babylonia. They decided to build a city and live there.

When most people built buildings, they used big stones. But these people decided to do something different. They made bricks and baked them until they were very hard. They used them to build their buildings. They thought they were pretty smart. Then, they came up with a plan that they thought would make them famous.

"Let's build a tower so tall that it reaches to heaven," they said. "Everyone will think we are amazing. Everyone in the rest of the world will talk about how powerful and wise we are!" They got right to work building their big tower.

But God was not happy with their plan. He knew if
they finished the tower, they would think they were
more powerful than He was. So God decided to stop
their work.

One day the people came to work on their tower, but they couldn't understand what one another was saying. God had made everyone speak different languages! Now they couldn't work together to finish the tower. That place was named Babel because that's where the languages of the world became all mixed up and confused.

WHat JESUS SaiD

Whoever makes himself great will be
made humble. Whoever makes himself
humble will be made great.
MATTHEW 23:12

God wants His people to love Him and trust
Him. But, He doesn't want anyone to think they
are smarter or more powerful than He is. When
people start thinking like that, God will always
put them in their place.

Jesus' words remind us to keep God in the
Number One spot in our hearts and never think
we are stronger, smarter, or better than God.
After all . . . He is God!

THE BIRTH OF ISAAC

Abraham and Sarah served God. They tried to always obey Him. They were both very old, and they didn't have any children, even though God had once promised them that they would have a big family. Sarah knew that she was too old to have a baby now.

One hot day Abraham was sitting outside his tent. Three strangers came walking by, and he invited them to sit down and rest. "Sit here in the shade. I'll get you some food and water," he said.

"Sarah, make some food for our guests," he called.
Sarah got right to work. She could hear the men
talking outside the tent. One man, who was the Lord,
said, "By this time next year Sarah will have a baby
boy." That idea was so silly that Sarah laughed to
herself. *That's not possible!* she thought. *I'm too old.*

"Why did Sarah laugh?" the Lord asked Abraham. "Is anything too hard for God?" Sarah wondered how he even knew she had laughed. Abraham didn't know what to say. God himself had come to give them a message.

By human standards, Abraham and Sarah were certainly too old to have a baby, but with God, anything is possible. About a year later Sarah gave birth to a baby boy, just as God said she would. They named him Isaac because that name means "laughter."

WHaT JeSuS SaiD

All things are possible
for him who believes.
MARK 9:23

Nothing, absolutely nothing, is too hard for God. When God says He will do something, He will do it! He had promised Abraham and Sarah a long time before that they would have a family. They had given up on Him keeping that promise. They should have believed.

We can trust God to keep His promises to us, too. Even (or especially) when something seems impossible, keep trusting God. He can do anything!

JACOB'S AMAZING DREAM

Jacob did something that made his brother, Esau, very angry at him. Their mother decided to send Jacob away before Esau hurt Jacob. She thought Esau would calm down if he didn't see Jacob for a while.

Jacob walked and walked. He was heading to Haran to stay with his uncle. He didn't know when he would ever come home again. When night came, Jacob stopped to rest. He found a smooth rock to use as a pillow. He stretched out to get some sleep.

While Jacob was sleeping, he had an amazing dream. In his dream, Jacob saw a big ladder. It was resting on the ground, but it was so tall that it reached all the way to heaven. Many angels were going up and down the ladder.

The most amazing part of the dream was that God was standing at the top of the ladder. God spoke to Jacob in his dream. He said, "I am the Lord, the God of your grandfather Abraham. Someday I will give you this land that you are sleeping on. I will always take care of you. I will be with you wherever you go."

Jacob felt better when he woke up. Now he knew that God was with him. He knew that God would never leave him and would always take care of him. Jacob promised, "I will give God one-tenth of all He gives me." Jacob took his stone pillow and stood it on end. He left it there to remind him of his amazing dream.

WHAT JESUS SAID

Your Father knows the things
you need before you ask him.
MATTHEW 6:8

Jacob may have felt a little sad or afraid to leave his home. He didn't have a job. He wouldn't be with his family anymore. He didn't know if he and his brother would ever be friends again. But, he found out that God promised to always take care of him. He didn't have to worry about anything, he just had to trust God.

Jesus wanted people to always remember to trust God to take care of them. He knows everything we need—even before we do! In fact, He takes such good care of us that sometimes He gives us things before we even need them!

JOSEPH FORGIVES

Jacob the grandson of Abraham, had many children. His favorite son was Joseph. Jacob even gave Joseph a fancy coat like rich people wore. This made Joseph's brothers angry. When Joseph had a dream about his brothers bowing down to him, well, that was the last straw.

"Let's get rid of Joseph. We can tell Father that a wild animal attacked him," one brother said. "No," said another one. "Let's sell him to some men who are going to Egypt. They can make him a slave." So, Joseph became a slave in Egypt. He worked hard, but when someone told a lie about him, he ended up in prison!

A few years later, the king of Egypt had an upsetting dream. God helped Joseph explain it to the king. That pleased the king so much that he made Joseph second in command of his whole kingdom! Joseph began saving food for the kingdom, because the king's dream said that a terrible drought was coming.

Sure enough, a few years later people were coming from everywhere to buy or beg food from Joseph. One day his brothers came to ask Joseph to sell them some food. He recognized them right away, but they didn't know him, until he told them who he was.

Joseph could have thrown them into prison. He could have sent them home with no food and let them starve. But Joseph did not do those things. "Don't be afraid," he said. "You meant to hurt me, but I forgive you. It was God's plan to save our family from starving."

WHat Jesus saiD

Forgive the sins we have done,
just as we have forgiven those
who did wrong to us.
MATTHEW 6:12

Throughout his whole life, Joseph stayed close to God. He tried to live the way God wanted him to live. That meant that he forgave those who did wrong things to him.

Jesus' words are from the prayer that Jesus used to teach His followers how to pray. His words show that there isn't any point in asking God to forgive our sins if we are not willing to forgive those who do wrong things to us.

The Birth of Moses

Jacob, also called Israel, moved his family to Egypt. There his descendants were known as Iraelites or Hebrews. They had many children and their numbers grew greatly. After many years, a new king began to rule Egypt. The Hebrew people became slaves and had to work long and hard. The king was afraid that the Hebrew men would form an army and take over his country. He ordered that all the Hebrew baby boys be killed at birth.

But one woman, who was the mother of a baby boy, decided to hide him from the soldiers. She hid him for three months. After that his cries were too loud to hide any longer. But, the woman did not want her son to die so she thought up a plan to save him.

While her daughter, Miriam, kept the baby quiet, the mother covered a basket with tar. When it was dry, they put the baby inside.

Miriam and her mother carried the basket to the river, hoping that no soldier would notice them. They tucked it in the tall grass on the riverbank. Then the mother went home, and Miriam stayed behind to watch over her little brother inside.

A little while later, the Egyptian princess came to the river. She noticed the small basket and sent a servant to get it. When they opened it, the baby was crying. "This is a Hebrew baby," the princess said. She felt sorry for him and decided to keep him. She named him Moses because that means "taken out of the water."

WHaT JeSuS SaiD

Your Father in heaven does not want
any of these little children to be lost.
MATTHEW 18:14

It is amazing to think that God has a plan for each of our lives. None of us are here by accident. Jesus' words remind us that God loves His children and doesn't want bad things to happen to any of us. Sometimes, He protects us by using another person. That's what happened with Moses! God used Moses' mother to keep the baby safe.

God had a job for Moses to do, and Moses was around to do it because his mother took a chance and protected her son . . . just like God wanted her to do. God will take care of each of us, too.

I Can't Do It . . . But God Can!

When Moses grew up, he left Egypt. He went to live in the land of Midian and became a shepherd. One day when Moses led his sheep to a field, something at the edge of the field caught his eye. It was a bush that was on fire, but was not burning up. It just kept burning. As Moses stared, he heard his name called, "Moses!" It came from the bush! "Here I am," Moses answered. "You are standing on holy ground," the voice said. Then Moses knew that God was speaking to him.

"I've seen the pain of my people who are slaves in
Egypt," God said. "I want you to lead them to
freedom." Moses could not believe this. "I can't. The
king of Egypt would never listen to me. Why would the
people even listen to me? I'm not anyone special."

"What are you holding?" God asked. "My walking stick," Moses said. "Throw it down," God said. Moses did . . . and it became a snake. "Pick it up," God ordered. Moses carefully grabbed the snake by the tail . . . and it became his walking stick again. "I will do miracles like this so the people will know that I am with you," God said.

Moses had one more problem. "I'm not a very good speaker," he said. God had an answer for this one, too. "I'll send your brother, Aaron, with you. I will speak to you. Then you will tell Aaron what to say." Moses had no more questions. He believed he could do the job because he knew that God would help him every step of the way.

WHaT JeSUS SaiD

Those people who know they have great
spiritual needs are happy. The kingdom of
heaven belongs to them.

MATTHEW 5:3

Moses knew that he could not do anything
without God's help. He wasn't even willing to give
the job a try until he was sure that God was going
to be there to help him. He leaned on God and
trusted God to help him do the job ahead.

A person who is full of pride is not very
useful to God. That kind of person thinks he is so
strong or wise or powerful that he does not need
God's help for anything. Jesus said that the
person who knows how much he or she needs
God is happier than the person who doesn't think
about that.

The Passover

God wanted His people freed from slavery in Egypt. He did some amazing miracles to convince the king to let the people go. Each time God did a miracle, such as turning water to blood or sending flies that covered the land, the king told Moses to leave with the people. But, when the problem stopped, the king changed his mind.

God sent nine different, terrible plagues to the people of Egypt. But, the king would not let the people go. Finally, God made plans for the tenth and most terrible of the plagues. The firstborn son in each Egyptian home would die.

God told the Israelites what to do to protect their children from this plague. "Take a perfect lamb. Cook it, and eat it with your family and neighbors. Take some of the blood of the lamb and smear it on the sides and tops of the doorframes of your houses."

"Wear your traveling clothes while you eat. Have your things packed and be ready to leave when I tell you." The people did what God said. The Lord passed through the land of Egypt at midnight. The firstborn son in each home died, even the firstborn of the animals were killed.

But no one died in the Israelites' homes where the lambs' blood was smeared on the sides and top of the doorframe. God passed over these homes. He told the people to always remember how He had protected them and kept their children safe on this night. From then on, the Passover was to be celebrated every year. That way, their descendants would always remember this great thing God had done.

WHat JesUS SaiD

God clothes the grass in the field . . . So you
know how much more God will clothe you.
Don't have so little faith!
Luke 12:28

God protected His people from the
tragedy of the tenth plague. He didn't lift them
out of Egypt and mysteriously transport them
to safety. He led them through the problem, and
He protected them from it.

God will not take us out of the problems of
the world—dealing with evil and dishonest
people. But, He will protect us and walk with us
through the problems. No one can take away the
hope of God's people. He promised to take care
of us—Jesus said so!

The Red Sea

"**G**et your people out of Egypt!" the king shouted. He was finally giving in after the ten terrible plagues hit his people. Moses led the Israelites out of Egypt. God showed them the way by traveling in front of them in a big cloud. At night the cloud turned into fire. They walked across the desert until they came to the Red Sea.

They set up camp there. But, as they got settled someone noticed a cloud of dust off in the distance. The people watched as the cloud came closer and closer. Finally, they saw that it was the Egyptian army! The king had changed his mind. He wanted his slaves back and sent his army to get them!

The sea was in front of them and the king's army behind them. How could they escape? They were afraid they were going to die right there by the Red Sea. But, Moses wasn't afraid. He asked God what to do, and God gave him a plan.

"Trust God! See how He will save you!" Moses told the people. Moses held his hand out over the water. That's what God had told him to do. A strong wind began to blow. It blew so hard that the water blew apart. There were two big walls of water with dry land between them.

The Israelites walked through the sea on dry land! When the Egyptian soldiers tried to follow them, the water crashed down on them. All the soldiers in the sea drowned, but every single Israelite got safely to the other side.

WHat Jesus saiD

God even knows how many hairs are
on your head. So don't be afraid.
MATTHEW 10:30-31

God cares about His people. But, the
Israelites forgot for a while how important
they were to God. They forgot that He would
protect them. They forgot about all the other
miracles God had done to keep them safe.

Jesus' words remind us that God knows us
so well that He even knows how many hairs are
on our heads! We can trust Him to take care of
us no matter what kinds of things we're facing!

FOOD FROM HEAVEN

The Israelites walked through the desert. It was hot and tiring, and they complained a lot. After two months, they began to worry about not having enough food. "It would have been better for us if you had left us in Egypt. We're going to starve to death in this desert!" they grumbled.

Moses did what he always did when the people
complained. He asked God for help. "I will send
food," God said. "Every night I'll send quail the
people can cook. Every morning I'll cause a special
bread to fall from the sky.

"The people can pick up enough food for each day. They shouldn't try to pick up extra food and store it. It will spoil and smell terrible!" Moses explained God's plan to the people. They waited to see how God would do it.

That night a big flock of quail landed on the ground. The people captured the birds and had them for dinner. The next morning when the people woke up, there was a heavy dew on the desert ground. When the dew dried up, white flakes were left. The people called this special bread manna—food from heaven. It tasted like wafers made with honey.

The manna stayed there until the sun got hot, then it melted. The people picked up enough manna to feed each person for the day.

Some of the people didn't listen to the rule about how much to pick up. They tried to save some for the next day, but it spoiled and stunk up the entire camp! God sent manna and quail to the Israelites for forty years! They didn't go hungry for even one day!

WHat JeSUS SaiD

Don't worry
about the food you need to live.
LUKE 12:22

God always took care of the Israelites. But every time they had a problem, they forgot all the wonderful things He had done for them before. If they had remembered this time, they would have known that they didn't need to worry about food. God would take care of them again.

Jesus' words remind us that we don't have to worry about anything. We are God's children and He will take care of us, no matter what happens in our lives. We can trust Him for food and clothing . . . for anything we need.

Ten Good Rules

God led the Israelites through the wilderness. He led them all the way to the base of Mount Sinai. The people set up camp while Moses went up on the mountain because God wanted to talk with him. God came down to the mountain to meet with Moses.

The people waited for Moses at their camp. They didn't know exactly what was happening up on the mountain. But when smoke covered Mount Sinai they became very scared. There was smoke because God came to Moses in the form of fire.

The mountain shook like a powerful earthquake was rocking it. The people were even more afraid. God said they weren't allowed to come up on the mountain, or even to touch it. If they did, they had to be put to death.

Only Moses was allowed to talk with God. God gave Moses some important rules to pass on to the people. God wrote these on two stone tablets. Five of the rules were about how they should get along with each other. The other five were about how they should respect God.

Here are the rules God gave Moses:

1. DON'T HAVE ANY OTHER GODS EXCEPT ME.
2. DON'T WORSHIP IDOLS.
3. BE CAREFUL HOW YOU USE THE LORD'S NAME.
4. KEEP THE SABBATH DAY HOLY.
5. HONOR YOUR FATHER AND MOTHER.
6. DO NOT MURDER ANYONE.
7. DO NOT BE GUILTY OF ADULTERY.
8. DO NOT STEAL.
9. DO NOT TELL LIES ABOUT ANYONE.
10. DO NOT WANT WHAT YOUR NEIGHBOR HAS.

The people said they would obey God's rules.

WHaT JeSUS SaiD

If you want to have life forever,
obey the commands.
MATTHEW 19: 17

God gave the Israelite people the Ten
Commandments to make life easier for them. It
helps to have rules as guidelines to live by. Jesus
knew that, too.

He reminded people that pleasing God
means obeying His commands.

We have the entire Bible now to help us
know how God wants us to live. Jesus said that
obeying God means we can live with Him forever
in heaven. That's a good reason to obey!

The Golden Calf

Moses was up on the mountain with God for a long time. "He's never coming back," the people began to say. "Maybe he ran away. Maybe he died up there." The people complained to Aaron that they needed a god they could see.

"Make a god to lead us," they said. "Bring all your gold jewelry to me," Aaron said. The people gave him all the gold they could find. Aaron melted the jewelry and formed the gold into the shape of a calf. "This is our new god!" the people said.

Aaron built an altar in front of the golden calf. He planned a special feast to honor the new god. The people danced and partied and gave offerings to the golden calf.

God saw everything that was happening. He was not happy. In fact, He wanted to destroy the people and start a new nation with Moses' descendants. "Wait," Moses begged. "Please don't destroy them. Give them another chance. You brought them all the way out of Egypt. Don't give up on them now!"

God listened to Moses. He decided not to destroy all the people. But, the people had to be punished for turning away from God, so Moses went back down the mountain. He melted the golden calf and ground the gold into powder. Then, he poured the powder into water and made the people drink it. They would never forget this punishment.

WHaT JesuS SaiD

Remain in me,
and I will remain in you.
JOHN 15:4

God doesn't want His people to worship anyone or anything else . . . just Him. So, when the people began to worship a golden calf instead of God Himself, that made God angry. He was so angry, He wanted to destroy His own people.

God should always be NUMBER ONE in our lives. It's very important that we never let anyone or anything become as important to us as God. If we stay close to God, He stays close to us! That's what Jesus was reminding us of when He said to "Remain in God." He was saying, "Stay close to God. Keep Him NUMBER ONE!"

Twelve Spies

The Israelites were ready to settle down and stay in one place. "I am giving you the land of Canaan," God told Moses. "Send one man from each tribe into the land to scout it out." Moses chose twelve men to sneak into Canaan.

Moses told the spies to see what kinds of crops grew in the land. He asked them to find out if the men there were big and strong. Moses also wanted to know if the cities had big walls around them.

The spies searched the land for forty days. They made sure that no one saw them. They found that good crops grew there. In fact, they picked some grapes to take back and show the people. The bunch of grapes was so big that it took two men to carry it.

When the spies came back, the people gathered to hear their report. "The land is good," they said. "Good crops grow there." Ten of the spies said, "The cities are big and have thick walls around them. The people are as big as giants. We wouldn't have a chance against them. We shouldn't even try to take the land."

But two of the spies—Caleb and Joshua—said, "God promised to give us the land. He will help us defeat the people. We don't have to be afraid." But the people didn't listen to them. They listened to the other ten and decided not to try to take the land. God was disappointed that they didn't trust Him. "You will wander in the desert for forty years," He said. "Because you did not trust Me to protect you, only Caleb and Joshua and your children will get to live in the land of Canaan."

WHat Jesus saiD

"Don't let your hearts be troubled.
Trust in God. And trust in me."
JOHN 14:1

God had promised the land to His people. That
meant that there wasn't any obstacle too big for
them to overcome. God would help them no matter
what. All the people had to do was trust Him and
have peace about the future. But they didn't.

We can have peace today. Jesus promised it to
us. We can have peace because He is with us,
helping us and leading us. There is no reason to be
afraid about anything or to worry about anything.
Peace comes from God. Fear and worry do not.

The Walls of Jericho Fall

After Moses died, Joshua led the Israelites into the land of Canaan. The people in Jericho were afraid because the Israelites were camped nearby. They had heard how God helped the Israelite army defeat its enemies. The people of Jericho closed the city gate and locked it up tight. No one went in and no one went out.

God spoke to Joshua, "I'm giving you the city of Jericho," He said. "Just do exactly what I tell you to do." Joshua obeyed. He led his soldiers in a march around the city of Jericho. The priests marched with them carrying the Holy Box. Seven priests marched in front of the Holy Box carrying horns. But none of the soldiers or priests said a word.

They marched around Jericho once a day for six days. The people inside Jericho didn't know what to think about this strange behavior. For the seventh day, God had different instructions for Joshua and the army. He told them to march around the city seven times.

They marched around the city once, twice, three times . . . again and again. The people inside Jericho didn't know what to think now. On the seventh time around, the priests blew their horns and Joshua commanded the soldiers to shout!

As they shouted, the big walls around Jericho began to crumble and fall. Joshua and his soldiers rushed into the city. They captured the people and took control of the city without even one battle! All they did was obey God's instructions.

WHat JeSuS SaiD

If your faith is as big as a
mustard seed, you can say to this mountain,
"Move from here to there." And the mountain will
move. All things will be possible for you.

MATTHEW 17:20

Who would think that the thick walls
around a city would crumble and fall down just
because some soldiers marched around and
shouted? Well, Joshua knew that anything could
happen if he trusted **God** to do what **He** said.
Joshua was right.

A mustard seed isn't very **big**, but even that
small amount of faith in **God** means that
incredible things can happen. Jesus said so! A
little faith grows more faith. Because when we
see what amazing things **God** will do for us, then
we trust **Him** more and more.

GiDeon's Little Army

Many years passed. Once again the Israelites forgot to stay close to God. This time the Midianites became their cruel enemy. A mighty warrior named Gideon called together an army to fight the Midianites. Many, many Midianite soldiers came, and they felt sure they could win the battle with such a big army. However, God had a different plan.

"You have too many soldiers," God said to Gideon. "I don't want your soldiers to brag that they won the battle themselves. Tell anyone who is afraid that they can go home." Gideon gave the soldiers this message and 22,000 men left. Now Gideon had 10,000 soldiers.

"You still have too many soldiers," God said. He told Gideon to take them down to the water. "The ones who drink water by scooping it up in their hands and lapping it up like a dog are the ones who may stay with you." That left Gideon with 300 soldiers.

Gideon took his 300 men down to the Midianite camp one night. He gave each soldier a torch of fire, a jar, and a trumpet. They quietly surrounded the Midianite camp. When Gideon gave the signal, the soldiers blew the trumpets and broke the jars that covered their torches.

They didn't even attack, each man stayed in his place. But when the Midianites saw the torches and heard the trumpets they were terrified. They ran around in circles and began fighting one another. Gideon's army won the battle without even fighting!

WHaT JeSUS SaiD

Everyone who makes himself great will be
made humble. But the person who makes
himself humble will be made great.

LUKE 14:11

God didn't want Gideon and his army to think
they were the ones who defeated the enemy. If
they thought that, they might become proud of
themselves and begin to think that they didn't
even need God. He made Gideon's army small so
that Gideon and his soldiers would depend on God
for the victory.

We get into trouble, too, when we start to
think we are important. We must always
remember that any strength, power, and success
we have comes from God.

Samson, The Mighty Man

Again the people of Israel did not obey God. So God let the Philistines rule over them for 40 years. Then God chose Samson to fight against the Philistines. God told Samson to never cut his hair. As long as Samson obeyed God, he had incredible strength. The Philistines hated Samson, and they wanted to capture him. A woman named Delilah agreed to help them. The Philistines would pay her lots of money to find out what made Samson so strong.

Delilah begged Samson to tell her the secret of his strength. "Tie me up with new rope, and I'll be as weak as anyone," he said. Of course, that was a lie. He broke the ropes as if they were string. Many times Delilah asked him his secret. And each time Samson told her a lie.

Then one day, Samson got tired of Delilah's asking and he told her the truth. "If my hair is cut, I'll be as weak as a baby." As soon as Samson fell asleep, Delilah told the Philistines, and they cut his hair.

Sure enough, Samson became weak and the Philistines dragged him to prison. They also hurt Samson's eyes. And Samson was never able to see again. Eventually, Samson's hair grew back and his strength returned, but the Philistines didn't know it.

One day the Philistines brought Samson to a big celebration, so the people could make fun of him. They stood Samson by the pillars that held up the roof. Samson prayed, "God help me once more!" Then he pushed on the pillars with all his strength. They broke in half and the roof came crashing down. The Philistines were all killed. Samson died, too, but he saved God's people as he died.

WHaT JeSUS SaiD

If anyone wants to follow me,
he must say "no" to the things he wants. He
must be willing even to die on a cross, and
he must follow me.

MATTHEW 16:24

Samson should have said "no" to Delilah. He should not have taken any chances about disobeying God. But, when he realized that he had done wrong, Samson asked for another chance. He was willing even to die himself, if he could serve God.

Jesus' words show that there shouldn't be anything more important to us than serving and following God. That means we won't always get to do what we want to do or go where we want to go. But the important thing is that we do what God wants us to do.

Loyal Ruth

A woman named Naomi, who was living in Moab, decided to go back to her home in Judah. She and her family had been living in the country of Moab because there was not enough to eat in Judah. Her two sons even married women from Moab.

When her husband and both sons died, Naomi had no family left except her two daughters-in-law. One day, she heard that the people back in her country now had plenty of food. And she set off for her home in Judah.

"I'll come with you," Ruth said. The other daughter-in-law, Orpah wanted to come, too. But, when they started to travel, Orpah missed her family too much. Naomi sent her home. She tried to send Ruth home, too. But Ruth said, "I want to come with you. Your people will be my people and your God will be my God."

When they got to Judah, Ruth had to find a way to get food for her and Naomi. She followed along behind workers in a field, picking up any grain they dropped. She and Naomi used the grain to make bread. It was hard work, but Ruth did it every day.

"Who is that woman?" asked Boaz, the owner of the field. He thought Ruth was very nice to take care of Naomi. Boaz fell in love with Ruth. They got married and had a baby boy named Obed. Ruth, Boaz, Obed, and Naomi were very happy.

What Jesus Said

I tell you the truth. Everyone who has left his home, brothers, sisters, mother, father, children or fields for me and for the Good News will get a hundred times more than he left.
MARK 10:29-30

Ruth left behind everything that she was familiar with. Her family, her hometown, her friends, even whatever religious faith she had grown up with was left behind. She went with Naomi and adopted her family and even Naomi's faith in God. Ruth's new walk with God was honored. He gave her a whole new family!

These words of Jesus are especially comforting to missionaries and Christian workers who leave their families behind to serve God in other countries. But, even for those who stay home—when we give our lives to serving God, He will reward us. We can never out-give God!

Hannah's Powerful Prayer

Hannah wanted to have a baby. More than anything, she wanted to have a baby. But she didn't have any children. Her husband understood, but other women made fun of her because she had never had a child. This made Hannah very sad.

One day Hannah and her husband went to the Lord's Holy Tent to worship God. When they were finished, Hannah prayed for a while by herself, "O God, please give me a child. She promised God that if He gave her a son, she would give the child back to Him to serve Him all his life.

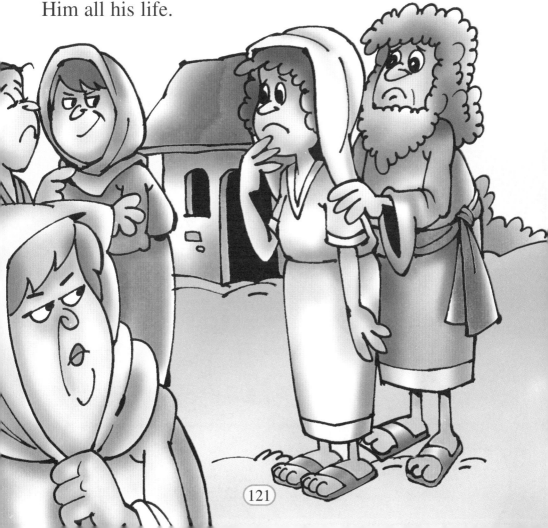

Eli, the priest, was in the Lord's Holy Tent. He saw Hannah crying, and he saw her lips moving, but no sound was coming out. He thought Hannah was drunk! "How dare you come into the Lord's Holy Tent when you are drunk!" he scolded her.

"No, I haven't been drinking. I've been asking God to help me with my problems," Hannah said. Eli saw how serious she was. "God will hear your prayer," he promised.

Sure enough, almost a year later, Hannah gave birth to a boy. She named him Samuel. That name meant that she had asked God for him. Hannah kept her promise to God, and when Samuel was old enough, she took him to the Lord's Holy Tent to live with Eli and learn how to be a priest.

WHaT JeSUS SaiD

Continue to ask, and God will
give to you. Continue to search, and
you will find. Continue to knock,
and the door will be open for you.

MATTHEW 7:7

Hannah wanted a child with all her heart.
She poured out her heart to God, and He heard
her request. He looked at her heart and saw
how very much she wanted to be a mother.

Jesus knew that we all ask for things
sometimes that we don't REALLY want. But,
when we continually ask God for something,
He looks at our hearts to see how much we
really want this thing. Then, He gives us what
will be good for us.

Samuel Hears a Voice

Samuel was just a little boy, but he didn't live with his mother and father. He lived in the Lord's Holy Tent with Eli, the priest. He was learning how to serve God as a priest. Samuel's mother came to visit him at least once a year. She always brought him new clothes when she came.

One night when Samuel was in bed, he heard his name called. "Samuel! Samuel!" Little Samuel jumped out of bed and ran to Eli's room. "Yes Sir, what do you want?" he asked. But, Eli had been asleep. In fact, Samuel woke him when he ran into the room.

"I didn't call you," Eli said. "Go back to bed." Samuel went back to bed. He had just gotten settled in again when he heard, "Samuel! Samuel!" He jumped up and ran back to Eli's room. "Yes, I'm here. What do you want?" he asked.

Again, Eli said, "I didn't call you. Go back to bed!" So
Samuel went back to bed. Then a third time he heard,
"Samuel! Samuel!" This time, when he woke Eli, the
old priest knew what was happening. He told Samuel
what to do.

"It is God calling you," he said. "When He calls again, answer 'I am your servant. Speak Lord.'" That's what Samuel did, and God told him many things that He was going to do in the future. This was the first time God had spoken to Samuel.

WHat JeSUS SaiD

A student is not better than his teacher.
But when the student has fully learned all
that he has been taught, then he will be
like his teacher.

LUKE 6:40

Eli was teaching Samuel everything he
could about serving God and an important
lesson about listening to God.

The best way for us to learn about God
and how to please Him is to know Jesus—our
teacher—better and better! If we stay close
to Jesus and follow His teaching, we will
become more like Him.

And this pleases God.

David Is Chosen

Samuel learned from Eli how to serve God. When he grew up, he became a prophet of God. His job was to do God's work and teach people about God. One day, God sent him to Bethlehem to see a man named Jesse.

"I have chosen one of Jesse's sons to be the next king of Israel," God said. "I want you to appoint the young man so that everyone knows he will be the next king. Go to Bethlehem and offer a sacrifice to God.

"Invite Jesse and his sons to join you." When Samuel saw Jesse's oldest boy, Eliab, he thought, *This boy must be the one God has chosen. He is handsome and tall.* But, God said, "No, this is not the one. Don't look at how handsome or tall he is. I don't look at his appearance; I look at his heart."

Jesse called his next son to pass by Samuel, but this boy wasn't the one God had chosen either. Samuel saw seven of Jesse's sons, but none of them were the chosen one. "Do you have any other sons?" Samuel asked. Jesse told him that his youngest son was back at home watching the sheep.

Samuel sent for the young boy. When David walked in, God said, "This is the one. Appoint him to be the next king of Israel." So, Samuel poured oil on David's head, and from that day on, God's Spirit was with young David, the future king of Israel.

WHAT JESUS SAID

Those who are pure in their thinking
are happy. They will be with God.
MATTHEW 5:8

Samuel made the mistake of thinking that the way a person looks shows how important the person is to God. It didn't matter that seven of Jesse's sons were tall or handsome or strong. God was much more concerned with what was in their hearts. He wanted a king who loved Him and would serve Him. David's pure heart is what God was looking for.

Jesus' words remind us that God looks at our hearts, too. We may be attractive on the outside. We may even say and do nice things, but if we don't love God and want to serve Him in our hearts, none of that other stuff matters.

A Small Light Shines Bright!

David grew up knowing that God had chosen him to be the next king. He always tried to live for God. One day David's father sent him to visit his brothers who were soldiers in King Saul's army. When David arrived at the camp, he heard one of the enemy soldiers making fun of King Saul's army.

Each day the giant soldier challenged the Israelites to send someone out to fight him. Goliath was nine feet tall and had a huge spear, and a man carried a big shield in front of him. The Israelite soldiers were scared of Goliath. They hid from him. But, David said, "I'm not afraid. I know that God is on my side. I'll fight him."

King Saul wasn't so sure. "You're just a kid," he said. "Goliath has been fighting many years." David convinced the king to let him fight by telling him the ways he had protected his sheep. "Okay, you can go," the king finally said. "But at least wear my armor." David tried it on, but it was so big that he could barely walk. He decided to fight Goliath his own way.

David picked up five small stones and went to meet the giant. When Goliath saw him coming, he got angry that the Israelites were sending a boy out to fight him. "Come on, I'll feed you to the birds!" he shouted.

"No way. God is on my side!" David shouted back. He dropped a stone into his slingshot, twirled it around over his head, and let the stone fly. It smacked Goliath right in the forehead, and the giant crumpled to the ground. David won! Well, actually God won!

WHAT JESUS SAID

Do you hide a lamp under a bowl or
under a bed? No! You put the lamp
on a lampstand.

MARK 4:21

David let his light shine bright! His faith in God was so strong that he knew he could trust God for anything. Some of King Saul's soldiers might have had faith in God, too, but they didn't let their lights shine. Their lights were hidden when they let their fear show. David knew that a secret faith in God wasn't much good. He let everyone know that he trusted God by letting his light shine bright.

We should let our faith shine bright, too. We can do that by letting everyone around us know how important God is to us—all the time!

Best Friends Forever

After David killed Goliath, King Saul invited him to live in the palace with the king's family. King Saul's son, Jonathan, soon became good friends with David. Prince Jonathan promised to always be David's friend. And to show his friendship, he even gave David his uniform, including his sword, bow, and belt.

David became famous all across the land for killing Goliath. People even made up songs about how brave he was. Before long King Saul was jealous because his people liked David more than they liked him.

After a while King Saul became so jealous that he wanted to kill David. He even tried to stab David with his spear. David ran away and waited for Jonathan to find out if King Saul was going to try again to kill him. Jonathan was sure that his father would not hurt his best friend. But, Jonathan was wrong. The king got angry with him for even asking about it. In fact, he threw his spear at Jonathan!

After that, Jonathan knew that David had to leave. He went to the field where David was hiding and gave him the signal they had agreed on. He shot an arrow into the field and told his servant to get it. When the boy ran to find it, Jonathan shouted "No, the arrow is beyond that spot."

Those words were the sign that David's life was in danger. He would have to go away. As soon as Jonathan sent the servant away, David came out of hiding. He and Jonathan were sad because they had to say good-bye. But they promised to be friends forever.

wHat JesUs saiD

Do for other people what
you want them to do for you.
LUKE 6:31

Jonathan lived out Jesus' words in this story. Two times in this story, he treated David in the same way he would like to be treated. He generously gave him gifts, then he saved David's life. King Saul's anger may have scared Jonathan, but Jonathan still treated David kindly—the way he would want to be treated. Many years later, David passed that kindness on to Jonathan's son.

Sometimes it may be hard for us to treat others the way we would like to be treated. We may be angry, scared, tired, or just feeling selfish. Jesus' words remind us to put those feelings aside and treat others with kindness.

Peacemaker Abigail

David stayed in the wilderness to keep away from Saul. He depended on the kindness of strangers for food. Nabal was a rich man. He owned lots of land and 3,000 sheep and 1,000 goats. He had a beautiful wife named Abigail, but Nabal was a mean and unkind man.

David heard that Nabal was cutting the wool from his sheep, so David sent some men to ask for food. The men reminded Nabal that David's men had protected him and his animals when they were camped nearby. They said, "During this happy time, will you share with us?" But, Nabal refused to help David. He even called him an outlaw.

When David's men told him what Nabal said, David shouted, "Get your swords! We're going after him." He planned to kill Nabal. Four hundred men went with David.

One of Nabal's servants hurried to Abigail and told her what her husband had done.

"David's men protected and helped us. Your husband should have given him food," the servant said. Abigail jumped into action. She gathered cooked meat and grain, bread and fruit. She told servants to pack the food on donkeys and head for David's camp. She followed them on her donkey. But she didn't tell Nabal what she was doing.

On the way Abigail met David coming to kill her husband. "Master, let the blame for my husband's actions fall on me," she said. "Everyone knows he is a mean man. I didn't know your men had come, or I would have made sure they got food. I've brought some for you now. Please accept it and spare my husband's life." Abigail stopped David from killing many people. He accepted her gift, and sent her home in peace.

WHAT JESUS SAID

Those who work to
bring peace are happy.
MATTHEW 5:9

Abigail was a peacemaker. She went out of her way to solve a problem that she had not caused. By being a peacemaker, she kept David from doing something terrible.

Peacemakers go out of their way to bring peace. They are able to explain things and calm down people who are upset. Jesus said that peacemakers are special to God. Keeping peace is one way of setting aside our wants and needs and helping other people instead.

DAVID'S TRUE COLORS

David spent the next few years running from Saul. He couldn't stay in one place very long because if Saul found him, he would kill him. Through all that time, David did not even say an unkind word about Saul. He even had chances to hurt Saul, but he chose not to.

One time some people told Saul where David was hiding. Saul and his 3,000 soldiers hurried to find him. They set up camp and waited for morning. David and his advisor, Abishai crept into the camp late at night. King Saul was sleeping in the middle of the camp, surrounded by his soldiers. But, no one had stayed awake to guard the king.

"Let me at the king!" Abishai begged David. He was eager to pay back Saul for all the trouble he had caused David. But David stopped Abishai. He wouldn't let his servant hurt the king. He knew that God Himself would punish Saul.

"Pick up the spear and water jug that are near where King Saul is sleeping," David said. They crept close to the sleeping king and got those things, then quietly left the camp. David went up on a hill across from Saul's camp and shouted to the soldiers. "Hey, you guys don't do a very good job of guarding your king!"

King Saul recognized David's voice. "I could have killed you," David shouted. "See, I've got the spear and water jug that were beside you. But, I would not harm the Lord's king. Why are you trying to hurt me?" King Saul said that he was sorry and that he wouldn't chase David anymore. But, he didn't mean it.

WHat JeSUS SaiD

Love your enemies.
Pray for those who hurt you.
MATTHEW 5:44

The way David treated King Saul is a good example of Jesus' command to love our enemies. King Saul tried over and over again to kill David. When David had the chance to hurt Saul, he refused. David didn't want to do anything to hurt the man God had chosen to be king. Over and over again David showed love and respect for Saul.

It's a natural reaction to want to hurt people who hurt us . . . but that's not what Jesus said we should do. Anyone can love their friends, but when we act like Jesus, we love our enemies.

David Shares His Riches

King Saul continued to chase David until he was killed in a battle. Jonathan was killed, too. David was sad when he heard they were dead. Then the people of Israel made David their new king, just as God had planned so long ago.

King David did a good job leading the people of Israel. His armies won many wars. David remembered the promise he made to Jonathan to always show kindness to his family. He asked his servant if any of King Saul's family was still alive.

He was told that Jonathan's son, Mephibosheth, was still alive. He was crippled in both feet. "Bring this man to me," David ordered. "I want to show kindness to him." Mephibosheth was afraid when David's servants came to get him.

"Don't be afraid," David said. "I want to be kind to you for your father's sake." Mephibosheth was amazed when David told him that he wanted to give him the land that had belonged to King Saul's family. Mephibosheth knew that King Saul had been mean to David. He thought David might punish him because of that.

David put Mephibosheth's fears to rest. "You are always welcome in my house. You are always welcome to eat at my table," he said. "I want you to feel that you are one of my sons." He commanded Ziba, a former servant of King Saul, to farm the land for Mephibosheth. David made sure Jonathan's son was taken care of.

WHat Jesus SaiD

If you cannot be trusted with
worldly riches, then you will not
be trusted with the true riches.
LUKE 16:11

As king of Israel, David had as much money and power as anyone could imagine. God knew that He could trust David to use those riches well. He certainly did that in this case. He could have hoarded land and riches and refused to help anyone—especially the grandson of the man who had tried so often to kill him. But David didn't do that; he was generous with all that had been given to him.

Jesus' words remind us that any riches God gives us show that He trusts us with those things. We should be generous with our money and things. Then we will have the riches of heaven someday.

A Wise Decision

When David got older, he made his son, Solomon, the king of Israel. Solomon was a strong leader who loved God. One night God came to Solomon in a dream and promised to give him anything he wanted. Solomon didn't ask for riches or power, he asked for wisdom. God gave him wisdom.

A while later two women came to Solomon with a problem. One woman said, "This woman and I live in the same house. We both had babies about the same age. Her baby died during the night. So, she took my baby and left her dead baby in my bed."

But, the other woman said, "No, she's lying. The live baby is mine and the dead baby is hers." Solomon listened to both women. Then, he sent his servant to get a sword. He had a plan that would help him know which woman was the real mother.

"Cut the baby in half. Give half to each woman," Solomon ordered.

The first woman quickly said, "No! Don't hurt the baby. Let her have him."

The second woman said, "Fine, cut him in half. If I can't have him, then she can't either."

"Give the child to the first woman. She is the real mother," Solomon said. He knew that the real mother would rather give the baby away than let him be killed. Solomon used the wisdom God gave him to make this decision.

WHat Jesus saiD

What a person says with his
mouth comes from the way he thinks.
And these are the things
that make him unclean.
MATTHEW 15:18

Solomon used the wisdom God gave him to understand that what the second woman said showed that in her heart she had no feelings for the baby. If she were the true mother, she would have spoken words of love for the child.

Jesus' words remind us that what we say speaks louder than what we do. Our words show what kinds of feelings are hidden deep in our hearts.

BREAD FOR ELIJAH

Many years later, a king ruled Israel who did not love God. Elijah was God's prophet at that time. He traveled around teaching people about God and helping them learn how to serve God. It was an important job.

God took care of Elijah . . . even when there was a terrible drought in the land and no one could find food. God told Elijah to go to the village of Zarephath. God said that a woman there would give him food. Elijah obeyed and went to Zarephath.

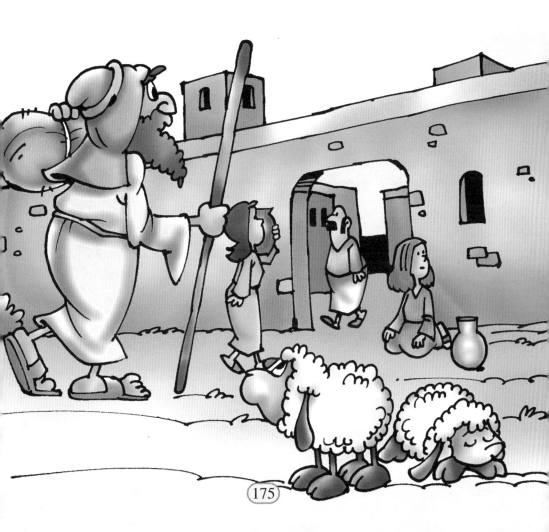

As he came into town, he saw a woman near the gate. "Could I please have a drink of water?" he asked. When she got up to get the water, he asked for some bread, too.

The woman sadly said that she couldn't give him bread. She only had a little flour and oil left to make a small loaf of bread. After it was gone, she and her son would starve to death.

"Go ahead and bake some bread for me. Your oil and flour will not run out," Elijah told the woman. "God will take care of you." The woman went home and did what Elijah said. He was right. No matter how much she used, her jars of oil and flour never became empty.

WHAT JESUS SAID

I was hungry, and you gave
me food. I was thirsty, and you
gave me something to drink.

MATTHEW 25:35

This poor widow of Zarephath served God by taking care of God's prophet Elijah. She believed what Elijah said and shared her food with him. God took care of her because she honored His servant Elijah.

Jesus' words remind us that we show our love for God by caring for people around us. When we share things to help other people, we show the love that is in our hearts.

A New Coat For Elisha

Elijah pleased God very much by the way he lived. So, God decided to take Elijah to heaven, even before Elijah died. The prophet who would take his place was Elisha. When it was getting close to the time for Elijah to leave, Elisha stayed close beside his teacher. He wanted to learn everything that Elijah could teach him about serving God.

"Elisha, stay here. The Lord wants me to go to Bethel," Elijah said. But Elisha wouldn't stay. He wanted to spend every minute with Elijah. They went to Bethel and to Jericho and then on to the Jordan River. At the river, fifty men came to see them. They stood off to the side to see what Elijah would do.

Elijah took off his coat, rolled it up, and hit the river water with it. The water divided! Elijah and Elisha crossed the river on dry ground. "What can I do for you before I leave?" Elijah asked Elisha.

"Leave me a double share of your spirit," Elisha answered. That was a hard request, but it came from Elisha's heart. So Elijah promised that Elisha would have it, if he saw Elijah leave.

When a fiery chariot zoomed down and took Elijah to heaven, Elisha saw it. Elijah's coat fell to the ground. Elisha picked it up and said, "Where is the Lord, the God of Elijah?" Then he hit the water and it divided, the same way as when Elijah had hit it. Elisha would now be God's prophet, just like his teacher Elijah.

WHAT JESUS SAID

Whoever obeys the law and teaches
other people to obey the law will be
great in the kingdom of heaven.

MATTHEW 5:9

There is no doubt that Elijah was great in God's eyes—God took him to heaven in a flaming chariot! Elijah served God well by teaching Elisha and others how to follow God.

Jesus' words remind us that it's important for us to obey God's laws and, whenever possible, to teach others to obey them, too.

WISDOM OF a CHILD

While Elisha continued his work of teaching people about God, an enemy army captured the Israelites. One little girl was taken from her family to be the slave for the wife of Naaman, a commander in the army. Naaman had a terrible skin disease. The little girl knew that Elisha could help him.

"I wish my master would go see Elisha, God's prophet. He could heal him," the little girl told Naaman's wife. When his wife told him what the slave girl said, Naaman gathered silver and gold to give as a gift to Elisha, and he left with his servants for Elisha's house.

Elisha's servants met Naaman at the door and told him, "Our master knows why you are here. He says that you should go down to the Jordan River and wash in it seven times. If you do that, you will be healed." Naaman was angry! He was insulted! He thought that Elisha himself should come out and talk with him! He thought he was important enough that he deserved personal attention!

Naaman was so angry that he decided to ignore Elisha's instructions and just go home. But his servants chased after him. "Master," they said, "if the prophet had asked you to do something hard, you would have done it. Why not try what he has said? Please just go to the Jordan River and do what he said. Just try it, please!"

Finally, Naaman turned around and went to the Jordan River. He went down into the water seven times. When he came out the seventh time, his skin was clear. He was healed! "Now I know there is no God in all the earth except the God of Israel!" he said.

WHAT JESUS SAID

You must change and become like little
children. If you don't do this, you will
never enter the kingdom of heaven.
MATTHEW 18:3

Naaman was a proud man. He was an
important man in the army, and he was used to
having people serve him and treat him with
respect. So, when Elisha just sent servants out
to talk with him, Naaman was insulted. He almost
let his pride get in the way of being healed . . .
and of knowing the true God!

Jesus' words remind us that we need to
trust God and obey Him, just as little children
obey and trust—without questioning and arguing.
We should not think we are too important or
special to do what God wants us to do.

"Just Veggies Please"

Many years after Naaman's healing, King Nebuchadnezzar and his army from Babylon captured the Israelites. Nebuchadnezzar took some boys from important Israelite families and put them in a training program to serve in the palace.

All the boys in training were given fancy food to eat. It was the same food that the king ate. The king thought he was being good to them. But a boy named Daniel and his three friends didn't want to eat that food. They knew it was unclean according to God's laws, and they didn't want to dishonor God.

"Please just let us eat something else," Daniel begged the man in charge. But the man was worried that the king would notice if Daniel, Shadrach, Meshach, and Abednego didn't look as healthy as the other boys. If the king noticed, he would punish the man.

"Just do a test," Daniel begged. "Give us vegetables and water for ten days. Then, see how we are doing. If we look sickly, we'll eat the king's food." The man agreed to Daniel's plan.

Ten days later, Daniel and his friends were healthier and stronger than any of the other boys. The guard agreed to let them stay on the vegetables and water diet. God gave the four of them great wisdom and a special ability to learn. They honored God, and He rewarded them for it.

WHat Jesus saiD

You should be a light for other people.
Live so that they will see the good things
you do. Live so that they will praise your
Father in heaven.

MATTHEW 5:16

Daniel loved God and wanted his life
to show honor and respect to God in all
that he did. So, at the risk of making the
guard angry, Daniel took a stand and let
his light shine!

We may sometimes have to make
tough choices, as Daniel did, in order to
let our lights shine. But Jesus' words
remind us that whatever we do, wherever
we go, our lives should bring honor to the
heavenly Father.

A Hot Time in the Kingdom

Awhile later King Nebuchadnezzar had a big golden statue built. It was 90 feet tall and 9 feet wide. He sent out a decree that when the people heard music play, they should bow down and worship the statue. Any person who refused to do so would be thrown into a blazing furnace of fire.

Most people obeyed the order, but three young men who were Israelite slaves refused to worship the statue. Shadrach, Meshach, and Abednego worshiped God, and they refused to bow to anyone or anything else. Someone reported them to the king.

Soldiers grabbed the three Israelites and brought them to the king. "Are you refusing to worship the statuc I had set up?" the king asked. Shadrach, Meshach, and Abednego answered, "You can throw us into the furnace. Our God can save us, but even if He doesn't, we will not worship the statue you set up."

"Make the furnace seven times hotter than normal!" the king ordered. The three men were tied up and thrown into it. The fire was so hot that the soldiers who threw them into it were killed. King Nebuchadnezzar sat down to watch the Israelites die. Suddenly he jumped to his feet and called for his aides.

"Didn't we put three men into the furnace?" he asked. They told him that was true. "Then why do I see four men walking around in the flames? One of them looks like an angel. Bring the Israelites out!" Shadrach, Meshach, and Abednego came out of the furnace. They were not burned at all—in fact—they didn't even smell like smoke! God protected His servants from the fire.

WHAT JESUS SAID

No one can be a slave to two masters.
He will hate one master and love the
other. Or he will follow one master and
refuse to follow the other.

MATTHEW 6:24

Shadrach, Meshach, and Abednego had a choice to make. They knew the punishment for not obeying the king's order. They could have publicly worshiped the statue and privately worshiped God, but they knew that wouldn't work. There is no room in worship for God and anything else. They made the right choice.

Jesus' words remind us that it's impossible to serve two different masters. God wants all our worship. And if we try to split our worship between Him and something else, we'll end up hating that other thing . . . or hating God. It's better to put our whole heart into worshiping God.

Lions With Locked Jaws

A few years after the three men survived the fiery
furnace, King Darius chose 120 governors for the land.
He put three men as supervisors over the governors.
One of those men was Daniel. The other supervisors
and the governors were jealous of Daniel because the
king was planning to put him in charge of the whole
kingdom. They looked for ways to get Daniel in
trouble with the king.

The plan they came up with was to use Daniel's faith in God to get him in trouble. Everyone knew that Daniel prayed to God three times a day. So, his enemies talked the king into making a law that people could only pray to him. Punishment for breaking the law was to be thrown into a den of hungry lions.

Daniel heard about the law—it was announced throughout the kingdom—but he didn't pay any attention to it. He kneeled beside his window and prayed, just as he did every day. That's exactly what his enemies were waiting to see. They ran to the king and insisted that Daniel be arrested.

King Darius knew he had been tricked, but he couldn't do anything about it. He tried to find some way around the law. But, it couldn't be changed, so he had to let Daniel be put into the pit full of hungry lions. "May your God save you," he said to Daniel.

The king was so worried about Daniel that he didn't sleep all night. Early the next morning he hurried to the lions' den. "My God protected me," Daniel called out. "He kept the lions' mouths closed so they couldn't hurt me." The king was so happy that he issued a new law ordering everyone in the kingdom to respect and fear Daniel's God.

WHat Jesus saiD

If anyone stands before other people
and says he believes in me, then I will say
that he belongs to me. I will say this before
my Father in heaven.

MATTHEW 10:32

There was no doubt who Daniel served. He knew that if he prayed to God, he was going to be thrown into the den of lions, but that didn't stop him. Daniel was determined to serve God, no matter what! God honored Daniel's courage and took care of him.

Jesus' words remind us of what's most important—honoring and serving God no matter who is watching. The reward for serving God publicly is a home with Him in heaven.

A Brave and Beautiful Queen

Esther wasn't very old when she won the beauty contest that made her queen of Persia. The king chose her from hundreds of girls. Her beauty and charm made everyone love her. But now Queen Esther had a problem . . . a serious problem.

The problem began when Haman, one of the
government leaders, decided that everyone should
bow down to him. Most people did. But one Jewish
man who happened to be Esther's Uncle Mordecai,
did not. That made Haman very angry, and he ordered
soldiers to kill all the Jews in the country.

"Esther, help us. You're the only one who can save our people," Mordecai said. But, no one—not even the king—knew that Esther was Jewish. Mordecai had told her to keep that information quiet. She was afraid that the king would be angry when he found out. He might order her death, too!

Esther thought for a long time about what she should do. Then she told Mordecai to have all the people fast and pray for her. "I'm going to see the king. He can have me killed for coming to him without being called. But, if I die, then I die." When Esther went to the king, he was glad to see her and held out his scepter to her. Esther invited the king and Haman to a banquet. At the banquet, she invited them to another banquet the next night.

The next night, in the middle of the good food and laughter, Esther told the king about Haman's evil plan. "He is going to kill me and all my people," she said. But the king ordered that Haman be killed for his evil plan. The Jews were saved because of Esther's courage and trust in God.

WHat Jesus saiD

Whoever tries to hold on to his life will give
up true life. Whoever gives up his life for
me will hold on to true life.

MATTHEW 10:39

Esther was very brave, wasn't she? She could have kept quiet about being Jewish. She could have let all her relatives be killed while she lived like a queen in a beautiful palace. But, she didn't. She took a stand for her people, and she trusted God for whatever happened. She was willing to die if necessary.

We may not have to risk our lives in order to give our lives to Jesus. But, we may have to risk popularity or money. Jesus' words remind us that giving our lives to Him will lead to a deep, fulfilling life that popularity and money cannot give us.

The Greatest Fish Story Ever!

Go to Nineveh," God told Jonah. "Tell the people there to stop sinning and live for Me." But, Jonah didn't want to go to Nineveh. He didn't like the people who lived there. He thought that God should punish them.

So, Jonah ran away from God. He got on a boat that was going in the opposite direction from Nineveh. "God will never find me here," he said to himself and drifted off to sleep. But, God knew where Jonah was. As the ship sailed onto the sea, God sent a big storm.

The wind blew and the waves crashed. The sailors were afraid that the ship was going to sink. They threw cargo overboard to make the ship lighter, but the water splashing onto the deck was sinking the ship lower and lower into the sea. Finally, the sailors woke up Jonah. "Pray to your God and maybe He will save us."

Jonah knew right away that the storm was God's way of getting his attention. "Throw me overboard and the storm will stop," he told the sailors. They didn't want to do that to Jonah, but they did want to save their ship, so they tossed Jonah into the water.

Immediately the storm stopped. Jonah didn't drown because God sent a big, big fish that swallowed him right up. Jonah sat in the belly of that fish for three days and thought about how he had disobeyed God. When he told God he was sorry and that he was ready to go to Nineveh, the big fish spit him out on the shore. Jonah went straight to Nineveh and told the people to obey God.

WHat Jesus SaiD

Don't judge other people, and you will not be judged. Don't accuse others of being guilty, and you will not be accused of being guilty. Forgive other people, and you will be forgiven.

LUKE 6:37

Jonah judged the people in Nineveh. He didn't want God to forgive them or save them. He thought he was better than they were. What Jonah forgot was that God wants to forgive everyone. He wants everyone to have a chance to obey Him. Jonah's attitude landed him in the belly of a fish. Yuck!

We need to remember Jesus' words, too. We should not judge other people or refuse to forgive others. We should never think that we are better than anyone else. Remember that God loves all people and wants all people to love Him!

A Special Birth

God sent the angel Gabriel to Nazareth of Galilee with a message for a young woman named Mary. "You are going to have a very special baby," the angel told Mary. "Your baby will be God's Son, and you will name Him Jesus." Mary was surprised but she said, "I will do whatever God wants."

Later the angel also appeared to Mary's fiancé, Joseph, and told him it was okay for him to marry Mary. Before the baby was born, Augustus Caesar ordered that all the people in the country be counted. Joseph and Mary had to travel to Bethlehem to put their names in a register to be counted.

When Joseph and Mary reached Bethlehem, the town was full of visitors, and there was no room for them in the inn. But the innkeeper offered to let them stay in his stable.

That very night, Mary's baby was born, surrounded by the animals in the stable. She wrapped the baby Jesus in strips of cloth and laid Him in the animals' feed box. Then something amazing happened in a field outside the town.

Some shepherds were there watching their sheep when suddenly an angel appeared in the sky. "I bring you good news that will bring you great joy," the angel said. "Today your Savior has been born in the town of Bethlehem." Then a large group of angels joined in singing, "Give glory to God in heaven, and on earth, let there be peace to the people who please God."

WHAT JESUS SAID

For God loved the world so much that he
gave his only Son. God gave his Son so
that whoever believes in him may not be
lost, but have eternal life.

JOHN 3:16

God had a plan. He wanted to make
a way for people to be able to live in
heaven with Him someday. That plan was
to send His only Son, Jesus, to earth to
teach people how to know God better.

Jesus was the fulfillment of this
verse—God's plan in action. We can
receive the gift of eternal life by
believing that Jesus is God's Son, and
accepting Him as our Savior.

Escape to Egypt

A special star appeared in the sky about the time that Jesus was born. Some wise men in a country far to the east saw it. They knew that the special star meant that the new king of the Jews had been born. They followed the star so they could find the baby and worship Him.

The star moved through the sky, leading them to Jerusalem. The wise men went to King Herod and asked where they could find the baby. Herod was not happy to hear about a new king. "Come back and tell me when you find the baby," he told the wise men. "I want to worship Him, too." But it was a lie. He planned to kill the baby.

The wise men found Jesus in Bethlehem when the star stopped above the house where He was. They worshiped young Jesus and gave Him gifts of gold, frankincense, and myrrh. Then God warned them in a dream not to go back to tell King Herod. So they returned to their homes a different way.

Meanwhile, an angel of the Lord spoke to Joseph in a dream. "Get up!" the angel said. "Take Jesus and get out of town. Herod wants to kill Him!" Joseph got up and took Mary and Jesus out of Bethlehem right then. They traveled to Egypt where they would be safe from Herod's soldiers.

Sure enough, Herod ordered that all the baby boys in Bethlehem who were two years old or younger be killed. It was a very sad time in Bethlehem. Joseph, Mary, and Jesus stayed in Egypt until the angel came back to Joseph and said, "It's safe to go home now. Herod is dead." Then the little family went home to Nazareth.

WHat Jesus said

God the Father has shown
that he is with the Son of Man.
JOHN 6:27

Jesus is God's Son. This is the first time
that God intervened in Jesus' life to protect Him.
God wanted to be sure that His plan could be
carried out. Many times throughout Jesus'
earthly life, God made it clear that He was with
Jesus. He answered His prayers. He helped Jesus
do miracles. And when Jesus' earthly life ended,
He raised Him back to life.

As we get to know Jesus better and better,
we will see how God was . . . and is . . . with Him.

Make Your Heart Ready

Before Jesus began teaching people or doing the work God sent Him to do, a man named John told people that Jesus was coming. John the Baptist was the son of Elizabeth and Zechariah.

John went out to the desert of Judea and lived there. He wore clothes that were made from camel's hair. He wore a leather belt around his waist. John ate locusts and honey.

"Change the way you are living because the kingdom of God is coming soon!" John preached. People came to hear what John taught. They told John about the sins they had committed, and he baptized them in the Jordan River.

The Old Testament prophet, Isaiah, wrote about John the Baptist when he wrote, "This is the voice of a man who calls out in the desert: 'Prepare the way for the Lord. Make the road straight for Him.'"

John was quick to tell people, "I baptize you with water to show that your hearts and lives have changed. But there is One coming after me who is greater than I am. I'm not even good enough to carry His sandals. I baptize with water, but He will baptize you with the Holy Spirit."

WHat JeSUS SaiD

You are the light
that gives light to the world.
MATTHEW 5:14

John knew what his job was—it was to tell people that Jesus was coming. He pointed people to Jesus. John was a light in a dark world that showed people the way to Jesus.

Jesus' words remind us that we have jobs to do, too. We are to be lights in our world by telling people about Jesus.

Standing Strong

Jesus grew up, but He had not yet started His work for God. Then the Holy Spirit led Him into the desert to be tempted by the devil. Jesus didn't eat anything at all for 40 days and nights. He was very hungry!

The devil came to Jesus and said, "If You are really the Son of God, tell these rocks to turn into bread." That would certainly give Jesus something to eat. But instead of giving in to this temptation from the devil, Jesus said, "It is written in the Scriptures, 'A person does not live only by eating bread. But a person lives by everything the Lord says.'"

Then the devil led Jesus into Jerusalem. He took Him to a very high place on the Temple and said, "If You are really the Son of God, jump off. The Scriptures say that God has put angels in charge of You. They will catch You and keep You from even stubbing Your toe on a rock."

Jesus answered him with Scripture again, "The Scriptures also say, 'Do not test the Lord your God.' " The devil tempted Jesus once more by taking Him to a very high mountain. He showed Him all the kingdoms of the world and said, "I will give You all these kingdoms if You will bow down and worship me."

Again, Jesus used Scripture to answer the devil, "Go away from Me, Satan! It is written, 'You must worship the Lord your God and serve only Him.'" The devil left then, and angels came to take care of Jesus.

WHat Jesus saiD

Love the Lord your God.
Love him with all your heart, all your soul,
all your mind, and all your strength.
MARK 12:30

Jesus' example and His words show
that it is very important to love God more
than anything else. Sometimes it's hard to
choose to serve God because the things that
tempt us are so appealing—just as they were
to Jesus. But when we love God with all our
heart, soul, mind, and strength, we'll put Him
first—ahead of all the things that tempt us.

Jesus showed us, by how He lived and
what He taught, that loving God more than
anything else is the best way to live.

A Giant Picnic

When Jesus started teaching and doing miracles, news about Him traveled around the land. People came from everywhere to hear Him teach and see His miracles. He was always surrounded by crowds.

One day Jesus was teaching on a hillside outside of town. Thousands of people gathered to hear Him. They were so interested that they sat and listened for hours.

Finally some of Jesus' followers came to Him and said, "Send the people into town so they can get something to eat." But Jesus had a better idea. "No, you feed them," He said. The disciples didn't have enough money to buy bread to feed all these people.

But one young boy in the crowd had five little loaves
of bread and two little fish. He offered the food to
Jesus. The disciples weren't sure what good that
small amount of food would do. But Jesus knew
what to do with it.

He took the bread and fish and thanked God for it. Then He gave it to the crowd of about 5,000 people. Everyone had all they wanted to eat, and there were twelve baskets of leftovers.

WHat JesuS SaiD

The thing you should seek is God's
kingdom. Then all the other things you
need will be given to you.

LUKE 12:31

The people in this story wanted to know
what Jesus taught about God's kingdom. But
they were so interested in what Jesus was
saying that they forgot about going home to eat.
It pleased Jesus that they wanted to know about
God, but He also knew they needed to eat, so He
fed them.

We can trust God to meet our needs, too.
But we must seek God's kingdom first and
foremost. When we do that, we can trust Him to
take care of things like food and clothes for us.

Jesus Walks on Water

Late on the same day that Jesus fed the 5,000 people, His disciples got in a boat to cross the Lake of Galilee. Jesus stayed behind to say good-bye to the people and spend some time praying. The disciples were out in the middle of the lake that night when a strong wind began to blow.

The disciples were afraid because the waves were splashing lots of water into their boat. They were worried that it might sink. In the middle of the storm, they looked out and saw someone walking on the water! "It's a ghost!" they cried. Now they were more afraid than ever.

But it wasn't a ghost; it was Jesus. He was coming to them. He called to them and told them not to be afraid. Peter wanted to be sure it was really Jesus. He called out, "Lord, if it's really You, call me to come out to You on the water."

"Come on," Jesus said. Peter climbed out of the boat and began walking across the top of the water! But when he noticed the waves and wind all around him, Peter got scared and immediately sank into the water.

"Help me!" he cried. Jesus reached out and caught Peter. "Why did you doubt, Peter? Your faith is too small," Jesus said. The storm stopped when they got into the boat. The disciples worshiped Jesus. They knew that He was truly the Son of God.

WHAT JESUS SAID

Have courage! It is I! Don't be afraid.
MATTHEW 14:27

Peter was fine . . . as long as he kept his eyes on Jesus. When Peter realized that he was in a scary situation, he sort of forgot that Jesus was right there with him and there was no reason to be afraid.

This is important for us, too. Jesus' words remind us that we are never alone. So, no matter what kind of situation we're facing, we never have to be afraid. Jesus is always with us, and that can take away our fear.

Jesus Loves the Little Children

Crowds of people followed Jesus everywhere He went. They wanted to see Him do miracles. They wanted to hear Him teach about God. People were very curious about Him.

(258)

Jesus was kept very busy answering questions and teaching about God. He hardly ever had time to rest.

One day some people came to hear Jesus teach. They brought their small children along. The parents just wanted Jesus to touch their children and bless them.

Jesus' disciples thought He was too busy to be bothered with children. They thought He had more important things to do. "Go away," they told the parents. "Don't bring your children around here."

Jesus heard what His disciples were saying. "Stop!" He cried. "Let the little children come to Me. God's kingdom belongs to people who have faith like these little children." Then Jesus took the children in His arms and blessed them.

WHAT JESUS SAID

I tell you the truth. You must accept
God's kingdom like a little child,
or you will never enter it.
LUKE 18:17

You're a child—what kind of faith do you
have? Children have simple faith. You believe
what the grown-ups you trust tell you. You
believe what the Bible says is true, too.

Sometimes when people grow up they
make believing in God too complicated.
Jesus' words remind us that part of believing
in God is having faith. We may not always
understand everything He says, but we trust
Him so we believe it . . . the way a child does.

"WHO IS MY NEIGHBOR?"

One day a man who was a teacher of the law asked Jesus how to live forever. He said, "I know the Scriptures say, 'Love the Lord your God with all your heart, all your soul, all your strength, and all your mind. Also, love your neighbor as yourself.'" He was trying to show that he was living his life in the right way. He didn't want to change. "But I wonder . . . who is my neighbor?" he asked.

To answer his question, Jesus told him a story. "A man was on his way to Jericho when robbers attacked him. They beat him up and stole his money and his clothes. They left him on the road, naked and bleeding. The man thought he was going to die.

"Then he heard someone coming. It was a Jewish priest! But did the priest help the hurt man? No. He crossed to the other side of the road. A while later someone else came by. It was a Levite, a Temple worker. Did he help the hurt man? No, he kept on going, too.

"Then another man came by. He was a Samaritan—a
man from a different country. When he saw the hurt
man, he felt sorry for him. He bandaged his wounds
and put him on his donkey and took him to an inn. He
took care of the hurt man. He even paid the innkeeper
to take care of the man after he left.

"Which man was a neighbor to the hurt man?" Jesus asked. The teacher knew that it was the last one who helped the hurt man. "That's right. So you go and live the same way he did," Jesus said.

WHAT JESUS SAID

Love your neighbor
as you love yourself.
MARK 12:31

This story shows how the Good Samaritan went out of his way to help the hurt man. He was on a journey, but he stopped and helped. He put the man on his donkey and he walked. He spent his money to help the man, too. He helped someone he didn't even know!

Jesus wants us to love other people as much as we love ourselves. That means that, just like the Good Samaritan, we go out of our way to help others. Even if it's hard . . . even when it's inconvenient . . . even when it costs us money and time. This is how we show Jesus' love to others.

A Lesson For Two Sisters

Jesus traveled from town to town, teaching people about God, healing sick people, even bringing dead people back to life. In one town, a woman named Martha invited Jesus to stay at her house.

When He arrived, Martha was busy in the kitchen cooking up a great dinner to serve Him. Martha's sister, Mary sat down beside Jesus and listened to His teaching.

Martha had lots of work left to do in the kitchen. She thought Mary should help her, but Mary didn't come. She just kept listening to Jesus.

Finally, Martha went to Jesus and said, "I've got a lot of work left to do and my sister isn't helping at all. Tell her to come to the kitchen with me and help me finish the work. Then, I will have time to listen to You teach, too."

But Jesus didn't do what Martha wanted. He said, "Martha, you are upset about too many things. Only one thing is really important and Mary understands what that is. Mary has made a good choice, and I won't take it away from her."

WHat Jesus saiD

Come to me all of you who are
tired and have heavy loads.
I will give you rest.
MATTHEW 11:28

Martha worked and worked and worried and worried. She may have been the kind of person who was always busy and always upset about something. But Mary understood that knowing Jesus as well as possible was more important than making a fancy dinner or any other work she could do for Him.

Sometimes we get so busy with home and school and sports schedules that we start to worry too much, just like Martha did. But Jesus' words remind us that He will take care of our worries if we'll just slow down our busy lives and take time to be with Him. That's the most important thing we can do!

The Son Who Left Home

A man had two sons. The younger son decided he wanted to leave home. He asked his dad for his share of the family inheritance. The boy took the money and left home. He moved far away to another country.

The son who left spent every bit of the money he had. He wasted it all in wild, foolish living. He didn't even have money left to buy food. He had no choice except to get a job. The only job he could find was feeding pigs. Finally, the boy was so hungry that he wanted to eat the pig's food. He realized that he had been very foolish.

One day as he was feeding the pigs, the boy started thinking about home. "I'm dying of hunger while my father's servants have plenty of food to eat," he said to himself. "Maybe I should go home and ask my dad to let me be a servant."

And that's exactly what the son decided to do. He set
out for home. When he got there, he would ask his
father's forgiveness for the wrongs he had done. He
would ask to be allowed to work for his father, just
like the other hired workers.

The son was still a long way from home when his father saw him coming. His father hurried out to meet him. The boy asked his father's forgiveness. He said, "I'm not worthy of being called your son anymore. May I please just work as a servant for you?" The father was so happy that his son was home that he forgave him and planned a big party. He treated him as a son, not a servant.

WHat Jesus saiD

If your brother sins against you
seven times in one day, but he says
that he is sorry each time,
then forgive him.

LUKE 17:4

The father in this story must have been very sad when his son left home. He must have been very hurt when his son wasted all the money he gave him. But he forgave his son and threw a big party to celebrate that the boy was home.

God's forgiveness is much like that of the father in this story. He quickly forgives us each time we come to Him and say we're sorry for the wrong things we do. Jesus' words remind us that we are forgiven and that we should be willing to forgive others over and over again—every time they ask.

A Little Man In a Tall Tree

Jesus continued traveling around and teaching people about God. One time He was going through the city of Jericho. As usual, a crowd of people gathered to see Him.

One of the men in the crowd was Zacchaeus, a tax collector. Everyone knew that Zacchaeus cheated people by taking extra money from them when he collected taxes. He kept the money for himself. He didn't have many friends.

As the crowd of people lined the street to see Jesus pass, Zacchaeus ended up in the back. He was so short that he couldn't see over the crowd and no one would let him squeeze to the front. Zacchaeus climbed up in a sycamore tree so that he could see Jesus go by.

Jesus looked up and saw Zacchaeus sitting in the tree. He stopped and called to him. "Come down, Zacchaeus. I want to come to your house." Zacchaeus scooted right down and took Jesus to his house.

The people complained because Jesus went home with the tax collector. But after talking with Jesus, Zacchaeus understood that he should stop cheating people. He even said he would pay back the people he had cheated by giving them more than he had taken from them. This made Jesus happy!

WHat JESUS SaiD

If you love me, you will do
the things I command.
JOHN 14:15

Zacchaeus was curious about Jesus, just
as the other people in the crowd were. Just
being curious about Him didn't change the way
Zacchaeus lived. When he spent some time
with Jesus and got to know Him, then
Zacchaeus wanted to obey Him. He showed his
love and respect for Jesus by obeying Him in
the way he treated other people.

We show our love for Jesus by obeying His
commands, too. When we do what He says,
our actions say we love Him and He is really
important to us.

Jesus Brings Lazurus Back to Life

Jesus was good friends with Mary and Martha and their brother, Lazarus. When Lazarus got sick, Mary and Martha sent for Jesus. They knew He could help their brother. But Jesus didn't come right away. He waited two days before heading to Bethany.

By the time Jesus arrived, Lazarus was dead. In fact, his body had been buried four days before. Someone told Martha that Jesus and His friends were coming, and she went out to meet Him. "Lord, my brother would not have died if You had been here." When Mary came out to see Jesus, she said the same thing.

"Just believe," Jesus said. "Your brother will live again. I am the resurrection and the life." Then Jesus asked to go to the tomb where Lazarus was buried. When they took Him to the tomb, Jesus cried.

Then He said, "Move the stone that covers the doorway of the tomb." Martha tried to stop Him. "There will be a terrible smell. Our brother has been dead four days!" she said. But Jesus insisted, so the stone was rolled away.

"Lazarus, come out!" Jesus called. Everyone was amazed when Lazarus walked out of the tomb, still wrapped in his burial clothes. He was alive! "Take the cloth off him and let him go," Jesus said.

wHat Jesus saiD

I am the resurrection and the life.
He who believes in me will
have life even if he dies.
JOHN 11:25

Jesus used this whole experience
with Lazarus to teach that people who
believe in Him will live forever. He
showed His power by bringing Lazarus
back to life.

The promise for us is that when we
believe in Jesus, we will live forever—not
on this earth of course—everyone will die
on this earth. But we have the PROMISE
of being in heaven with Jesus forever.
What could be better!

Ten Men Healed

Jesus was on His way to Jerusalem when ten men stopped Him. All ten of them suffered from a terrible skin disease called leprosy. It was very contagious, and people who had it were forced to leave their homes and live together in villages.

"Jesus, please help us," the men cried. Jesus answered them, but maybe not in the way they expected. He said, "Go and show yourselves to the priests."

All ten of the men took off running toward the Temple. As they were running, each of them noticed that their skin disease disappeared. All ten men were healed!

One of the men, a man from Samaria, turned around and went back to Jesus. He loudly praised God for healing him. He bowed at Jesus' feet and said, "Thank You, Jesus."

Jesus looked around for the other nine men. But none of them came back to thank Him. "Is this Samaritan the only one who came to thank God?" Jesus asked. Then He told the man to get up. "You were healed because you believed."

WHAT JESUS SAID

Your faith has made you well.
LUKE 17:19

Ten men asked Jesus to help them. Ten men wanted to be well. Jesus healed all ten of them, but only one of them showed that he had true faith. Only one man recognized that Jesus had healed him. Jesus told him that his faith was the reason he was healed.

It's important for our faith to grow stronger and stronger. Remembering stories like this, where someone's faith was the reason they were healed, helps our faith grow. Remembering how God has worked in our lives in the past helps our faith grow, too.

Four Good Friends

When Jesus came to Capernaum, a big crowd gathered to hear Him teach. The house where He was teaching got so crowded that not one more person could get inside.

Four men came to the house, carrying a friend who was paralyzed. They tried to get their friend to Jesus, but the crowd of people wouldn't let them through.

But the friends didn't give up. They carried their friend up to the roof of the house. They started pulling away tiles to make a hole in the roof. Soon the hole was big enough to fit their sick friend on his mat through it.

The determined friends lowered the mat with the paralyzed man on it down into the room—right in front of Jesus! The people in the room must have been very surprised!

Jesus saw that the four friends had a lot of faith in Him. They truly believed that He could heal their friend. So, Jesus looked at the paralyzed man. "Your sins are forgiven," He said. "Pick up your mat and walk." The man did just what Jesus said! He picked up his mat and walked out of the house!

WHat Jesus SaiD

This is my command:
Love each other.
JOHN 15:17

These four friends showed real love for their sick friend. They each had to stop whatever they were doing to take their friend to Jesus. Then, when they couldn't get through the crowd, they had to come up with Plan B. They risked the anger of the owner of the house when they made a hole in the roof. They did all of this for their friend and because they believed Jesus could heal him.

It's easy to say that we love our family and friends. But real love sometimes takes some effort. It might mean doing things we don't want to do. It might mean taking time from the things we like to do in order to help someone else. That's real love.

The Last Supper

Jesus was in Jerusalem with His twelve followers, and it was time to celebrate the Feast of the Passover. He sent two of them to prepare the meal in a room on the second floor of a house in the city. Later Jesus and His twelve followers gathered there to celebrate the Passover.

Jesus knew that it was nearly time for Him to die. He wanted this last supper with His followers to be very special. He wanted them to understand what was going to happen to Him.

Judas, one of the twelve followers, was planning to do something bad to Jesus. He was going to lead some soldiers to Jesus. They would arrest Jesus and put Him on trial. Jesus knew what Judas was planning. "One of you is planning to turn Me over to my enemies," He said.

Everyone wanted to know who it was. "It's the one I
give bread to," Jesus said. Then He handed Judas a
piece of bread. "Do what you are planning to do," He
said. Judas left right away. The others didn't know
what to think.

After that, Jesus gave thanks for the bread, broke it into pieces and passed it out to His followers. Then He took a cup of wine and thanked God for it. He shared it with His followers, too. He said, "When you eat bread and drink wine, always remember Me."

WHat JesUS SaiD

Do this to remember me.

LUKE 22:19

Jesus knew that the end of His life on earth was very close. He wanted to be sure that His followers didn't forget Him. He wanted them to remember all the things He had taught them about living for God and loving each other. The bread and wine would be reminders that Jesus loved them enough to die for their sins.

These are the same things Jesus wants us to remember when we eat the bread and drink the fruit of the vine in the Communion Services of our churches. Remember that Jesus died for your sins—but He didn't stay dead. He came back to life, and you can someday be with Him in heaven forever!

Jesus and The Cross

After the Passover Feast, Jesus and His followers went to the Garden of Gethsemane to pray. While they were there, Judas came with a group of soldiers. They arrested Jesus and led Him away. His followers scattered because they were afraid.

A trial was held by some of the religious leaders. They hated Jesus. They did not believe that He was God's Son. They wanted Him to die on a cross. The religious leaders took Jesus to Pilate, the Roman governor. Pilate did not think Jesus should die, but he decided to give the people what they wanted.

Jesus was taken to a hill outside of town. The soldiers forced a man named Simon to carry Jesus' cross. Jesus was put on the cross, and the soldiers waited for Him to die. Some people made fun of Him. "If He is really God's Son, let Him save Himself!" they said.

Some of Jesus' friends were there, too. They were very sad. Jesus had never done anything wrong, but He was dying for the wrongs of all people everywhere. That's how much He loved people. About noon the whole land became dark. The darkness lasted for three hours. Finally, Jesus cried out, "Father, I give You my life!" Then He died.

A man named Joseph asked if he could take Jesus' body and bury it. The soldiers let him take it. Joseph wrapped Jesus' body in a cloth and took it to a tomb that had never been used before. The soldiers rolled a big rock in front of the opening of the tomb. They put a guard beside it.

WHaT JeSUS SaiD

The greatest love a person
can show is to die for his friends.
JOHN 15:13

Jesus came to earth, lived and taught, then died. All of that was part of God's plan to make a way for people to be able to live in heaven with Him. Jesus agreed to the plan. He died to pay for our sins—the bad things that all people do. Jesus had never done anything wrong. He gave His life because He loved us. That's the best love of all!

Jesus wanted His followers back then to understand how much He loved them. He wants us to understand that, too.

The Best News Ever!

Jesus died and was buried on Friday. Early on Sunday morning, some women came to the tomb where He was buried. They brought spices and perfumes to put on His body. That was the custom when someone died. But they couldn't do it on the day He died because it was the Sabbath and they had to rest.

The women were surprised when they got to the tomb.
The big stone was rolled away and the tomb was open!
They went inside the tomb, but Jesus' body wasn't
there! The strips of cloth that had been wrapped
around His body were lying there.

Suddenly two shining angels were standing in front of them. The women were frightened. The angels said, "Why are you looking for a live person here where the dead people are? Jesus isn't here. He has risen from the dead—just as He said He would!"

The women ran back to town to tell Jesus' other
friends that He was alive! Mary Magdalene stayed
behind. She saw a man that she thought was the
gardener. "Where have you put Jesus?" she asked.
The man turned to her and said, "Mary." It was
Jesus. He was alive!

Meanwhile, the other women told the disciples that Jesus was alive. Peter didn't believe what the women said. He hurried to the tomb as fast as he could and ran inside. The women were right—Jesus was gone! Jesus was alive!

WHat JeSUS SaiD

The Son of man must suffer many things.
He will be rejected by the older Jewish leaders,
the leading priests, and the teachers of the law.
The Son of Man will be killed. But after three
days he will be raised from the dead.

LUKE 9:22

Jesus is alive! His enemies had Him killed. They buried Him and guarded the tomb. But they couldn't win. God is more powerful than anyone or anything. He brought Jesus back to life, just as He had promised. Jesus' friends saw Him, so they knew for certain that He was alive.

Jesus is in heaven today, just waiting for His children (that's us!) to join Him there someday. We know that all of us will die someday—at least our human bodies will die. But we won't stay dead because God has power over death. He will bring our spirits to heaven to live with Him forever!

Breakfast With Jesus

Jesus appeared to His disciples several times after He came back to life. One time some of them were fishing on the Lake of Galilee. They fished all night but didn't catch anything. Early the next morning Jesus appeared to them. But they didn't know it was Him.

"Fish on the right side of the boat," He said. When they did, they caught so many fish that they couldn't pull them all in. They knew then that the man who told them where to fish was Jesus. They joined Him on shore for a breakfast of cooked fish.

After breakfast, Jesus asked Peter a question. "Do you love Me, Peter?"

Peter said, "Yes, Lord, You know that I love You."

"Take care of My lambs," Jesus said.

Jesus asked Peter a second time, "Peter, do you love Me?"

"Yes, Lord," Peter said. "You know that I love You."

"Take care of My sheep," Jesus instructed.

Then, Jesus asked a third time, "Peter, do you love Me?"

Peter was a little hurt that Jesus kept asking the same question over and over. "Lord, You know everything. You know that I do love You!" he said.

Jesus said a third time, "Take care of My sheep. Follow Me."

WHaT JeSUS SaiD

Go everywhere in the world.
Tell the Good News to everyone.
MARK 15:16

Every time Jesus asked Peter if he loved Him and Peter answered that he did, Jesus gave Him a job to do. Jesus had just died for the sins of all people, and He wanted all people to know that. He told Peter to get busy taking care of His sheep—sharing the good news of Jesus' love for people.

Peter had a special job to do for Jesus, and so do each of His followers. Each of us can share the news of God's love in special ways. Some sing beautifully, some write good stories, some people are good at being helpers, friends, or sending cards. We should always be looking for ways we can tell people about God's love.

Index of Bible Stories

Index of Bible People

Index of Bible Places